P9-EGB-543

We Love Babies!

Jill Esbaum

NATIONAL GEOGRAPHIC
WASHINGTON, D.C.

Big or tiny,

fast or
s-l-o-w,

smooth or bumpy,

short or …

We love **snouts**

and **bills**
and **beaks,**

bendy **trunks**

and **whiskered cheeks.**

Ears that **flop**

or stand up **tall** ...

ears we cannot see at all!

We love **stripes**

and **jazzy speckles,**

coats with **lots** and **lots of freckles.**

Fins and scales

and fancy **feathers.**

Paws and claws
and little flippers,

feet that look like **fuzzy slippers.**
Itty-bitty hooves and **toes.**

Webby footsies? We love those!

We love babies!

Yes we do!

We love **crawlers**,
playful **pouncers**,

swimmers,

climbers,

danglers,

bouncers.

We love **snuffles,**
snorts, and **cheeps,**

squawks and **baaaaas,**

yips and peeps.

Got a **hiccup** in your **moo?**

We don't care.

We love that too!

In **desert dens**
or **deep blue seas,**

in **farm**

or **forest families,**

alone or in a **snuggly pile,**

in a **herd**

or **single file** ...

MEET THE BABIES!

GREYLAG GOOSE
(gosling)

LION
(cub)

TWO-TOED SLOTH

AFRICAN ELEPHANT
(calf)

COMMON DORMOUSE
(pup)

CHEETAH
(cub)

GARDEN SNAIL

RED-EYED TREE FROG

PARSON'S CHAMELEON

SHETLAND PONY
(foal)

HUMPBACK WHALE
(calf)

INDIAN FOX
(pup)

CARIBBEAN FLAMINGO
(chick)

PURPLE SWAMPHEN
(chick)

ASIAN ELEPHANT
(calf)

HARP SEAL
(pup)

LOP-EARED RABBIT
(kit)

LONG-EARED JERBOA
(pup)

AMERICAN ALLIGATOR
(hatchling)

ZEBRA
(foal)

SERVAL
(kitten)

GIRAFFE
(calf)

CHINESE STRIPE-NECKED TURTLE
(hatchling)

ANGELFISH
(fry)

KILLDEER
(chick)

BLACK BEAR
(cub)

38

MANATEE
(calf)

POLAR BEAR
(cub)

INDIAN RHINOCEROS
(calf)

MOUNTAIN GORILLA

DOMESTIC DUCK
(duckling)

LEOPARD GECKO
(hatchling)

RED FOX
(cub/pup/kit)

HIPPOPOTAMUS
(calf)

RACCOON
(kit)

ORANGUTAN

WESTERN GRAY KANGAROO
(joey)

WILD BOAR
(piglet)

DONKEY
(foal)

BAY-WINGED COWBIRD
(chick)

MEW GULL
(chick)

DOMESTIC SHEEP
(lamb)

GROUND SQUIRREL
(pup/kit)

BONOBO

DOMESTIC COW
(calf)

MEERKAT
(pup)

ORCA
(calf)

ALPACA
(cria)

INDIAN TIGER
(cub)

PRAIRIE DOG
(pup)

GOLDEN SNUB-NOSED MONKEY

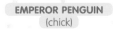

EUROPEAN BISON
(calf)

EMPEROR PENGUIN
(chick)

GIANT PANDA
(cub)

If a baby
animal is called
a special name,
it is shown here.

For Bria, William, Lawson, Bennett, and Leo —JE

Published by National Geographic Partners, LLC, Washington, DC, 20036.

Designed by Julide Dengel
Illustrations by Sydney Hanson

The author would like to thank the following people for making this book possible: Marfé Ferguson Delano, Lori Epstein, Julide Dengel, Molly Reid, Gus Tello, and Anne LeongSon.

Library of Congress Cataloging-in-Publication Data

Names: Esbaum, Jill, author. | National Geographic Society (U.S.)
Title: We love babies / by Jill Esbaum.
Description: Washington, DC : National Geographic Kids, [2020] |
  Audience: Age 2-5. | Audience: Pre-school, excluding K.
Identifiers: LCCN 2019007818| ISBN 9781426337482 (hardcover) |
  ISBN 9781426337499 (hardcover)
Subjects: LCSH: Animals--Infancy--Juvenile literature.
Classification: LCC QL763 .E83 2020 | DDC 591.3/92--dc23
LC record available at https://lccn.loc.gov/2019007818

Printed in China
19/PPS/1

PHOTO CREDITS:

Front cover, Klein and Hubert/Minden Pictures; back cover (UP), Norbert Rosing/National Geographic Image Collection; (CTR RT), Willi Rolfes/BIA/Minden Pictures; (LO), Suzi Eszterhas/Minden Pictures; 1, Sam Trull; 2 (UP), Dominique Delfino/Biosphoto; 2 (LO), imagebroker/Alamy Stock Photo; 3 (UP), Marion Vollborn/BIA/Minden Pictures; 3 (LO), John Daniels/ARDEA; 4 (UP), Kitchin & Hurst/Kimball Stock; 4 (LO), Ingo Arndt/Nature Picture Library; 5, Frédéric Desmette/Biosphoto; 6-7, Tony Wu/Nature Picture Library; 8, Sandesh Kadur/Nature Picture Library; 9 (UP), Claudio Contreras/Nature Picture Library; 9 (LO), Gianpiero Ferrari/FLPA/Minden Pictures; 10, gnomeandi/iStockphoto/Getty Images; 11, Ingo Arndt/Nature Picture Library; 12, Aflo/Nature Picture Library; 13 (UP), Valeriy Maleev/Nature Picture Library; 13 (LO), Science Source/Getty Images; 14, Tony Heald/Nature Picture Library; 15, Suzi Eszterhas/Minden Pictures; 16, Olivier Born/Biosphoto; 17, Matthijs Kuijpers/Biosphoto; 18, Gerry Yardy/Alamy Stock Photo; 19, shootnikonrawstock/Nature Picture Library; 20 (UP), Suzi Eszterhas/Minden Pictures; 20 (LO), Eric Baccega/Nature Picture Library; 21 (UP), Eric Baccega/Nature Picture Library; 21 (LO LE), ZSSD/Minden Pictures; 21 (LO RT), Suzi Eszterhas/Minden Pictures; 22-23, iStockphoto/Getty Images; 24 (UP), Bruno Cavignaux/Biosphoto; 24 (LO), Fabrice Cahez/Nature Picture Library; 25, ZSSD/Minden Pictures; 26 (LE), Heiko Kiera/Shutterstock; 26 (RT), Suzi Eszterhas/Minden Pictures; 27, Jurgen and Christine Sohns/FLPA/Minden Pictures; 28 (UP), Bruno Mathieu/Biosphoto; 28 (LO LE), Klein & Hubert/Nature Picture Library; 28 (LO RT), Gabriel Rojo/Nature Picture Library; 29 (UP), Tom Vezo/Minden Pictures; 29 (LO), Stonemeadow Photography/Alamy Stock Photo; 30 (UP), ClassicStock/Alamy Stock Photo; 30 (LO), Fiona Rogers/Nature Picture Library; 31, Nathan Allred/Alamy Stock Photo; 32 (UP), Thomas Dressler/Ardea; 32 (LO), Tony Wu/Nature Picture Library; 33 (UP), Adrian Sherratt/Alamy Stock Photo; 33 (LO), Michael Nichols/National Geographic Image Collection; 34 (UP), Juergen & Christine Sohns/Minden Pictures; 34 (LO), Thomas Marent/Ardea; 35 (UP), McPhoto/Pum/Alamy Stock Photo; 35 (LO), Klein & Hubert/Nature Picture Library; 36-37, Lisa & Mike Husar/Team Husar

Think we're finished? Hold it, friend.

There's one more thing we love ...

The End.